CON FIR MAT ION

BIAS

First printing

Published by Metatron Press
1314 Ave. Lajoie
Montreal, Quebec
H2V 1P5

www.metatron.press

Editor | Domenica Martinello
Cover design | Marcela Huerta

Library and Archives Canada Cataloguing in Publication

Title: Confirmation bias / Ivanna Baranova.
Names: Baranova, Ivanna, author.
Description: Poems.
Identifiers: Canadiana 20190161760 | ISBN 9781988355191 (softcover)
Classification: LCC PS3602.A72 C66 2019 | DDC 811/.6—dc23

Metatron Press gratefully acknowledges the support of the Canada Council for the Arts, which last
year invested $153 million to bring the arts to Canadians throughout the country.

Canada Council   Conseil des arts
for the Arts   du Canada

CODY,

THANK YOU SO MUCH
FOR READING TONIGHT.

I LOVED YOUR WORK
AND THINK YOU'RE
SUCH A GEM. PLEASE
BE IN TOUCH, BB !!

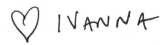 IVANNA

CONFIRMATION BIAS

IVANNA BARANOVA

Metatron Press

CONFIRMATION BIAS

1

2

3

4

5

confirmation bias
noun

the tendency to interpret new evidence as confirmation of one's existing beliefs or theories

"Belief is the social translation of desire." — Bernard Stiegler

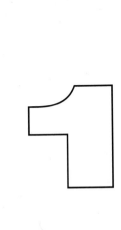

glow stick

somewhere in me
exists
a so-called
original urge
to align
with the astral
body
   but then
i see
all planetary
anatomy
aspiring
to life eternal
among the galaxies
regardless
   home to u-turns
cultural autopsies
and finite
emancipations
of this social
imaginary
   but baby
if not
hopeful
then really
what

should i be?
   notice
to eclipse
green lights
in these americas
i will
have to
learn to run——
   what else
should i think
about motion?
   your face comes
to memory
like a slow
collision
thus the traffic
of desire
awake again
in its daily
insurrection
   yesterday
i felt free
in a way
i could not
explain
then today
my thoughts
exhaust

their own
resolve
   ask
are my feet
planted firmly
to the——
where are my feet
in relation
to the——
why is the ground
against
my——
what is the cause
of this
flick flick
flickering?
   another day
and closer yet
to the final click
of the proverbial
dimming glow stick
such that
in the morning
stardust blooms
my guatemalan
apogees
and the hours
just go on

flowering
  hello
relentless garden
standing
in my heart's
early window
  watch with me
the sun
beams down
in the same
direction
it burns
  what else
is there to do
but witness
this world's
precarious
devotion?
  funny
it's not
always the eye
that's black
but rather
the rings
that surround
the iris
  refracting
and refracting

the careful glimmer
of this endless
ordinary
implosion

overture

melodic contact
tends to prioritize
the implosive——
the self-directed fuck
fuck fuck

which brutalities
cannot be obfuscated
by the referent   masculine
oblique

spiritual value
is not contingent
on the capacity
to produce
generate
or arrange
thought

gradually
any single moment
is a movement
an overture
can carry

tolerance

there's a quiet
    in my head   i can't
turn on

numb

the act
derives
value
through
its expression
and reifies
this value
through
the value
of that which
is expressed

milk

i think
this must be
one of the bad
times yet
when i touch
myself
every feeling
i've ever loved
simultaneously
beating

once
a man
or some
gray woman
with flailing arms
said we could play
a game where
every love
scene
is a feeling
recuperated
or an infinitude

it was so beautiful
i felt

my heart
quivering there

but the grass disgusted me
the house disgusted me
my body disgusted me

i have
enough regrets
but with you
where we crouch
love it's too cold to smoke

drinking coffee
trying to vomit
and drink
milk
pour the milk
burn

seattle

the smell
of   acetone
a translucent
turquoise summer

outside fritos
warm beneath sun

chlorine and lake
marinade my lungs

in the pool   bathroom
stall
my thighs
land on
the   spill of someone
else's piss

my soul
a small seven

acid

the rain's acid   here

i get wet   in
places
i didn't   plan to
before
growing

now what

i'm sad
in   the present
because
i am grieving
the future

i am
grieving   the future
because
it is
coming

i know
it is   coming
because
i have

been there—
breathing

used to be
i was
flowing   with love

now what
now what
am i flowing with

pacific

in game
theory
the brain
becomes
a pool
toy
when
drowning
floating
encompasses
everything
in the ocean
i breathe
your body
like a
life source
the grip
of trauma
vanishing
in lucid
oxygen
expanding
i touched
you
in water
where

we swam
once
we searched
resilience
and our bodies
became free
the industrial
park
a planet
blue very
blue
articulating
our sexual
credibility
getting it
right and
right
and right

organic

fidelity
is exhausting
and not
for the faint-hearted

the facade
of it creates
the intimidating task
of bashing your head
against the wall

        you don't have to
        agree

in your opinion
what does it mean
to be organically released?

        arbitrary?
        oversubscribed?
        fantastic?

no one puts
hetero
love acts
in a
drawer

hey

what are you   anyway?
some kind
of

dyke?

condition

that you find
ways
to sexualize
me
in even
the smallest
of time's
expanses
is what
gets me
thinking
of god
as a last
resort——
some
impossible
   vacation
like the lingering
sun tans
the brown
skin veils
the body
i never
wanted
but
on which
i must
depend

domestic idiot

most situations
are a test
of powerlessness

i don't control
the stakes
of your
disengagement

get it?

i don't control
the stakes
of anything

i don't mean
to suggest
you own me

but when you
put it like
that

electric hand

i.

our so-called friend
is gonna murder
the 10pm catcaller
who sits
in the chlorinated
tub

splash splash

two assholes
duking it out
over their
perceived ownership
of pussy

ii.

"take notes for the poem"

iii.

when in water women
are the starfish vigilante
of the aquatic panopticon

(habit-turned-necessity)

hot jet corners
soaked thighs
quiver
      drip no no (no)
rapt in pools of
masculine compulsion

iv.

my cells shimmer like
capricorn moon(stone)
crystal on a ring around
the ring around
my fat femme finger
that is mine
all mine

v.

_____? (how many) rituals
enacted "somaticize"
safety?

_____? (how many) crystals
ingested "ritualize"
the body?

vi.

"your arms
look strong
like they could
punch someone"
i say

recalling
the time my
own arms failed me
and i couldn't get away

sometimes
my electric hand
stays clenched in a fist
remembering

halfway

i want
to reply
about it all
when
you message me
at 3am
about
the grasshopper
on your
toothbrush
   our pacific
lake at
night
   your father's
smug face
in   the water
some guilt
   that year
in   rosh
hashanah
you brought
home
the 200 lb
burger boy
and i peed
on   the living

room floor
  i was
thinking
of you
on the bus
ride
first days
of school
  i didn't know
if i'd
make it
home
  i didn't know
i would
make it
home
  i ran
to the bathroom
the one
with   the stained
glass windows
  where i got
my   period
for the first
time
  i have
wanted
to be honest

just not
confessional
    i guess
it's time
i try

· ekg

everyone exalts
their own abject
plans this weekend
but my mind's
social trajectory
is invariably
same
i take up
smoking again
to confirm
our compatibility
a salve
for the disconnective
impulse
you know
my body
can't help
but dance
when i see you
on the platform
radiant somatic emblem
mirroring
these atomic
depths of me
congratulations
on your face

it's a good one
i plagiarize
your essence
as a means
of revival
so in life's
every iteration
witnessed
there's you
all this time
and still
i'm shocked
by loneliness
displayed
in myself
misunderstanding
the stages
of dispersal
and manifestation
i see now
i was an obdurate
rain in this urban
suburb
i discovered
how free
i felt when
i stopped
taking cover

i resurrected
in the alcohol
of perfume
i said yes
to not saying no
i was communicating
with dusk
and intimately
the sky
saturated me
in its omniscient
magenta enclosure
i couldn't help
but blush
and just like that
i became
gratitude's
fullest expression
i carried
my heart's
choreography
on an 8x11 sheet
i looked around
and forgot
what had been
taken from me
as soon
as i stopped
keeping score

cognitive

a sonata
leaks
a honda's
passing
speaker
and through
my jeans
i feel
a stochastic
throbbing
with celestial
urgency
emerge
look
up at the half
beaten sun
when
i arrive
i arrive
a waterfall
and how
like water
i become
love's equal

interstate

everywhere   can look

like
home

from the window
of   a bus

on   a highway
at night

you could be

in   any city

on
earth

better god

because i love
you   it is
            urgent

to inflict
this no-channel
grief
the body
will   eventually
like a splinter
reject

the planet's
obscene countdown
a forward   t-ta-task

last night
they shot a shopper
on   the third floor
of our
t-tiny   target world

ugh

to lessen dread
lesson   dead dead

you know i'd rather
be in a crib

in your life
there is a   melting
symposium i call quiet

a place
that is good
like a better god
gets   to be able
to get gotten

in all of ever
i was only   one night
or   day away
from this
sudden revival

revived
i   learned
that memory
is   an island

and how incredible
     the island's moon
     and the stars' moon
looked in their alikeness

not like
before   but rather
like   becoming
became
our common
  future fantasy
  unrequited

my mind's new york
is always winter

how i am   some blue orb
flashing   your phone
map's
morning
road   devoted

how i   cut the orb
with forward   motion

more light   in the window
more light   blocks the moon beam
blocks the glare   of our obedient
    design's   desire

we don't know
where   the longing
came from

only
that it   existed

we don't know
how
these things
happened
only that they   did

there's a tinge
on everything
about
this future
and   it always
fades just when
we arrive

neon

notice me
allowed
to lie quiet
on top
the concrete
if and
i want to
sure

you always
want to be
the fucking foucault
of public spaces

not here

of late
i know all
conversation
is a long arrival

to be close
to you and also
also further

us this erratic night
us this neon moon

mouth speaks nice
temperature tonight
then silence

the word
enacts itself
unconsciously i obey

pisces

smoking a cigarette
in the dark
9mg of melatonin
melt beneath
my tongue

nausea

i don't
even get
how it
happened
like this
then
remember

"the material
conditions
warrant
the psychic
phenomena"

nausea
of missing
you
fractures
my heart's
wholistic
intent

the parts
of me
that know
how to

love you
do

they
wake up
wanting
you
wondering
how
you've been

flash

if you entrust
me a task make
it opulence

        i flash upright
        wake a smile
        in nighttime's
        gentle heat

i guess i was
i guessed i was
      "emoting"

        in memory
        non-ecstatic
        only certain
        social
        exemptions
        are allowed

i made
obsession
of your promise
and that's
why
i had to call

i obsessed
myself
with obsession's
promise
and that's
why
i had to call

        before
        i could
        guarantee
        action
        i had to
        establish
        a pattern
        of wanting

        before
        i could
        establish
        a pattern
        of wanting
        i had to
        guarantee
        a legacy
        of emptying

the problem
with your
future
is it casts
a shadow
on this
living

like cut
the light source
drain the flowers

          i'm sorry
          for the things
          i said

          i went
          for a walk

          and now
          i feel
          better

eternal

nature
only becomes
serious
upon misremembering
your place
within it

be no one's
mother

make heaven
of every object

eternalize
yourself

azul

there's like
this weird
window
of time
where
i know
i have to
grieve
her
before
the eventual
worst case
scenario
  but even
grief
is a form
of insufficient
affirmation
  i thought
at least
of death
i could be
afraid
on my own
terms
yet still be

beloved
unconditionally
   these days
i can grieve
anyone
in the grey
brooklyn
streets
and still
remain
partly
beloved
at least
   to catch
her breeze
i walk where
the wind
path
must cut
through
me
   then up
and when
i'm
gone
a way
of knowing
she is
with me

is to
dream
  a part of
her staying
shines
  voice eternal
singing angel
baby
  to love
someone
so much
you
hear them
in the
sound
of things
  lately
every sound
becomes
our song
  tengo una
muñeca
de vestido
azul
  zapatitos
blancos
camisón de
tul

alarm

on the road
no cars exceed me

no pants
no destination
only small alarms

losing you
doesn't
make me
sad
necessarily

i just
think

we used
to do
those things

and now
we
don't

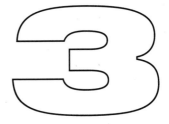

fire season

"don't miss anyone while you're drunk"

somatic

today passes through

and nothing

in the affirmative settles

> to exalt me in the right ways
>
> is a task whose criteria
>
> gets lost

talking it through doesn't help

but apparently this is how

feelings gone unfelt

gateway grief

when i get hit

i don't fall

i hover

how panic

suspends

the body

how the breath

adheres itself

to any promise

of motion

how the eye dilates

in peripheral

light's expanse

　　searching

　　for the yes in anything

habitually

you are camouflaging

yourself

in the affirmative

let me mourn

why don't you just

algorithm

the habit
always
dies
before
the
impulse

afterlife

i just can
not afford you

i get a grasp
on   my projected
suffering

know the raw
        syncopations
of my acceptive self

the body   you know
is a site
of opportunity
when   angled
correctly

gut check——
these are
my   "genuine" "feelings"

how to
        mention
the metaphysical
without wanting
to tape

the mouth of it
how to
tape
the mouth of it
then watch
the mouth
     become it

hello   mother life force
i've had
a "psychedelic" "experience"

you are not
interested   in me

you are
interested   in my shadow

how costly
it is
to need nothing
want   no one
incessantly
as i do

the   dull
ontological
ache

of my sexual capital
enacted

no   my sorrow is erotic
no   my fantasy subverts itself
no   my afterlife   is not a product
              of   your enrollment

i sweat myself
like   a loving dog
cum on the shampoo
towel
     and it's
     ecstatic

my siren   my affection song
     my coinstar at the
          corporate rave

i encountered
in   all corners
of my mind
some ephemeral
     past self
  i tried to make
  fantastic

you text me   "i feel it"

and the negation goes
dis-
solving
i get a grasp
on   my projected
suffering

and without   turning
instinctively
i know it's
you

aloe

how can i

ask you

to max me

out in a way

that's edgy?

the favor

being both a kind

of "fuck you"

and a "you complete

me baby"

at best

how to be

your new

translucent

heaven

given my

low gleam

in this eternal

rhinestone

aptitude

of the white

imagination

sorry

i lose

and make the money

spend the money

become

the money

all so

you'll keep me

in your pocket

like aloe-infused

kleenex

like cash cash cash

in this emergent

corporate utopia

everything shines

green

like that

even the mornings

reek of lime

even the shitty cacti

reverberate

emerald

no recourse

non-financial

non-carbonated

non-clean

lately

we discuss

capital

in the act

of fictive

ascension

incanting

the ungettable

these days

has anyway

become

my vague

little brand

of heaven

late night

in my fantasy
i refer to you
exclusively as
"you bitch"

you tell
me

just do it
just do it

so
i do it

like a bandaid
like a bandaid

on the late night
talk show in my head
i'm the latina jimmy fallon

bros love me

they bump my fist before
and after i take
the stage

drool congratulations
on each other
regarding
their guns dicks cars

discussing
the model make year

the state of capitalism's
boring neoliberal yawn
fantastic

gaba

easy just we drug
up to hex
out preservations
of fronts
gone conjured
or in the conjuring
toward our negligent
destruction so delicious
milligramming gaba
like so
the threat
of self-perjury
looming many ways
transparent
when i lean close
made out are the discrete
frequencies of the audition
tape in your mind
awaiting exceptional
review tho always
few stars
from your social
gods boo hoo
charmed you witness
every gesture orbit
half speed

chasing emblems
of your postured erasure
in starlight tho
you learn
they don't bless
the non-blessed
won't guess
your hesitations
or memorize
your door codes
leave now
or cut and run
who fails you?
who makes you
the martyr?
who asks you
to be so unshakeable?
i pray ruminative filth
so to protect you
by habit
by necessity

voicemail

no regret

to have dialed

remember dialing

dialing

remember you

as a feeling

a number dialed

a tone

      as static

electric

lisbon imagined

during
our sad little breakfast
by the window
we discuss
the patterns
in population density
of the last cities on earth
we've never been to
but know how to pronounce
the cities
we know how to pronounce
sparkle
and furthermore
don't enact any symptomatology
of "dependency"
or "interpersonally destructive behavior"
this is why
we like to imagine ourselves
inside of them
but not inside
the bodies of the people
who inhabit them
i make eye contact
with you
then suicide myself
into the sour cream

as if to say
i have arrived
again i am making it
about me
always about me
when i think of june
my body remembers
all of its lifetimes
i think
if i was in love then
i am not now
i think
if we love
each other again
i'll invite you
hopscotching
across the viaduct
with me
when we cross
back into the city
i promise to take you with me
whenever i go wherever i go
in this scenario
you don't ask me what's the prognosis
we fly to pronounceable cities
on fresh passports
wash the salt stains from our shirts
in hotel lobbies

opt out of infinite regress
opt out of pushing ourselves
off every ledge
for sport

solar return

yes
it's sad
now

but
think
of the sun

how
it will shine
tomorrow
on you

and every
beautiful
thing
that exists

opera

all the sorry
face plants
of the day
never
last long
despite
aphorisms
thrashing
cyclically
like the slow
coin dry
imagining
philly again
i'm reminded
of your receding
hairline
inching farther
from your face
day by day
and so i smile
but hey
my trichotillomania
your air jordans
the south end "Q"
mazel tov
taking turns chanting

emergencia!!
emergencia!!
in that operatic
drone
half a decade
cuts up
and apparently
it's good
to see you get
where you're
going
ripping apart
tuesday condoms
in the nick of time
hushing gaygaygay
like mouth roof clicks
safe bet soft serve
another
dollar menu
morning
USA
up against
the boring
calamity
of each
sunday's
inevitable collapse
wishing

the window
would open
wishing
the car
would start
just something
to mute
the tinnitus
gutting us
thru and thru
anything
to dull
the idyllic
shimmer
of everyone else's
everything else

gesture

i shine
a light
        to every
        atom
that surrounds
you

joy
recalls
my obsolescent
heart

powerade

the other day
on a small dirt trail
in alberta
i lost
balance
i fell down a cliff
my body landed
in the bow
river

i call charlotte
during the after
and in the afraid

she says to consider
the possibility
of existential dizziness
as a catalyst for falling
into the river

as a catalyst
for slow dying
blah blah

i am wet
and also i am tired

of considering the possibilities

i am just like the women
in all the other poems

tired   wet considerate

to say
i know some things
is a way of saying
i know many things

fuck me
and the stale
intellectual tendency

this is about
the kilogram
of mdma
rick had manufactured
before it was criminalized

dedications
from the underground
packed in little swiss bags
filled with little lab capsules
no labels

i am high on mdma

i am in a bed
and i am high on mdma

there is a
blue acid blanket
of porta potty chemicals
jumping the taste buds
on my cold red tongue

i spit purple
blend my jaw

i am presiding
over a chorus of angels

you
are the most
beautiful person
on earth and i love you

i say to the image
of my sister

                          who floats
                    inward then away

i dissolve

i am a metonym
            or is it metronome
            or is it mimetic mimetic device

i identify
with one word
at the expense of possible
identification with all other words

every mouthful
betrays me

sync up

            sync out

dissolve   dissolve dissolve

a boy i love tonight
holds his palm to my chest
to push the breaking further in and in and out

i am high on mdma on a saturday night
and i am not at the party

i am high on mdma on a saturday night
and i unbecome the party

powerade
pour another acid
blanket on my tongue

powerade
pour another acid
blanket on my tongue

tuck me in
with the chorus
of angels
ok

i love you

and you are the most
beautiful person
on earth

switch

dark comes

afraid
of the dark

light comes

afraid
of the light

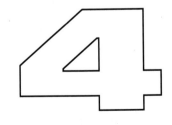

lucifer bitch

to dilute

corporeality

i go real

hysteric

hacks over

the sink

edging

the manic

instinct

i wanna

touch

your face

but depression

detests

anything

with a size

or shape

so instead

i inhabit

your body

as an

electrical signal

love you

like a time

of day

when i sell

myself

on the internet

i feel lucid

when i buy

myself

on the internet

i feel lucid lucid

i know

what

you would

say

regarding

moralism

shut up

you lucifer

bitch

funds

i know now
but didn't know then
that the most insidious
part about loving you
specifically would be
the incessant
replication
of every
nausea
ever
felt
like
grade five
hallway pissing
like standing too close
to the chevron pump like
sweating thru another
and another
once-clean
shirt
loving you is walking
down the sidewalk
to find myself
suddenly
staring
straight into
the eyes of a shitting dog

unable to look away
it being too late
loving you
isn't a relief
it's not romantic
it doesn't cause me
to believe in the divine
potentials of circumstance
instead
it's like waiting
in line forgetting
why i went to the store
in the first place
sliding my card
into the chip
reader too
fast too
fast
too
slow
trying
again and
again and
saying
to the cashier
i'm so sorry
i know
there's money
in my account

ziploc

you
easily any
provocative
configuration
of your boyish
5mg self

today feeling
fuchsia

tomorrow maybe
blue

ANOTHER
GORGEOUS
MORNING
ON THE
WEST COAST
OF AMERICA

winking at the clock 4am
clutching menthols
pepsi
a ziploc bag
of benzos

pantomime

you're
a beautiful
and devastating
thing

chasing
every false
sensation

fucking
the
glimmer
of every
star

sophia

just cause
the house
got torn
down
doesn't
mean
i forgot
you
quiet
flipping
pages
the rose
washed walls
taste of your
cum
that night
you wore
too much
blush
but i didn't
say so
instead
i unhooked
your bra
on the dance
floor
like a
pro

revelation

here in canada
we exit soft
no rush

shower
head
still
running

hand in our
open pants

tongue
on the door

some days
you epiphanize
every facial
contortion
you see

thinking
person x
will notice
a revelation
in you

but to me
you are
a revelation

to me
you are

lidocaine

i know
i can't tell
anyone my mantra
but it's my secret
to manifest
a belligerent
euphoria
that makes clear
the thing
worth looking
forward to is you
we hinge
on dark side
roof at dawn
what a night called sky
would call the future
one preposition
at a time
i'm a bus ticket baby
awaiting direct deposit
my mutable body
seeks enchantment
thru ridiculous
geography
like when the mental
block travels

my unconscious
my heart
beats faster
through each hour
of the night tis morning
the brightest dead
end i know
is dawn
i need
new strategies
to understand death
as departure
from escape room
chronology
looping images
to help
pass the minutes
breathe i know
i have to
make money
i know i have to save
to afford
the train to work
and back
it's financial surrender
running figures
to supply
the auto-renewable

numb
when my day's final
voice marks
its arrival
i arrive
through you
take up talking
about lidocaine again
about that hospital
off cherry
where i was sick
for fifty times
you didn't ask
about the context
but i described
the medicine
how it steeped
my veins
until i earned
back a working
consciousness
but also forgot
my name
a tyranny
of the body entity
entity atmosphere
atmosphere engendering
the sunrise thoughts

meet real time insomnia
like a cold
complimentary towel
i hover
the buy now button
on the discount
airline page
like here comes
stupid fucking nietszche
again diligently
haunting my large
and larger debt
illuminating the failings
of some coming era
like ha ha
all these memories
that won't integrate
even after a decade
what a decade
what a victorious win
for all the women
of the world
out here womening
over their things
and stuff
don't tell me
it's not a big deal

i ask my heart
to trust the authority
of its experience
and can see
it's not the precedent
of your relentless
apathy
that restates
my wanting
but the transitive
rigidity of your tone
there's a ceremony
out here
for everyone
even you
i'd risk psychosis
and vomit
if it's what ought
to be my psychic hope
that's my beloved rodent
in the garden
that's my mother
in the sky
of course i hate
when you speak
conclusively
of course i love
how you never do

water signs

i don't wanna mention death
any more than we obligate
thoughts of weather

whatever daily obituaries
and fahrenheit levels
consume us both

our bras cupping
pools of sweat

no matter the weather
no matter the month

when the temperature drops we go
coffin shopping at the colour house

we cruise control the drive home
so to sidewalk stare at the faces

that house the eyes of the expressions
of the people who do not love us now
didn't love us then
and never will

because we don't know any better

we chalk phenomenological consequence
up to the effects of obligation

conflate all intersectional theory
with lawlessness

proselytize lazy idioms about
astrology and the occult

when i joke about being garbage
it is because i am a joke about being garbage
and garbage is as garbage does as garbage does

isn't it amazing
the pithy fuckery
of the one-two conflation
to which i subject you

to make you
to make you want me
to make you want to touch me

wanting is the melting of the ego
wanting is the witnessing of melting
melting can be spontaneous and a-romantic
can tend to occur during the onset of any cycle

menstrual
psychiatric
or otherwise

just so you know:
when i want something
i ask for it

i never ask for you

5

mint

wow
what an honor
to even
have a place
to call
your graveyard
some final
emotional internship
in the search
for earthly
belonging
i went looking
to replicate
my dreams
in normative
motion
placating
bodily needs
thru nature's
continuous touch
i railed soft
mint essence
of a forest's
early scar
i was looking
for a different

outcome
my mortal
orbit
always
exhausting
itself thru
breathing's
confused
production
knowing
growth
is the natural
interpretation
of transcendence
knowing
transcendence
is compatible
with failure
knowing
failure
necessarily
takes the form
of devotion

problem

how
can it be
too much if
it's what
i feel

color therapy

tell me about your day mariana
about the song you shazamed
on the grocery store radio
the spilled bottle
that soaked the concrete
floor in a color
you called
cerulean
tell me
about the sauna
the baseball game
the blackhead strips
the incremental growth
in your backyard garden plot
mariana
i'm watching
the moon from the concrete
floor of this city park
the air is getting cold
but i'm calibrating
with a can of seltzer
cause for better or worse
i always run unbearably
pink and hot
i can't remember
the last time i looked at the sky

forgot how effortlessly
the clouds move
like without force or premeditation
drifting in unison
then dissipating
into small abandoned dots
i spent an hour
searching for the most plush
and verdant grass
where i could go to be with you
but it all just turned up dry
mariana i don't need good
only better news
i'm stuck in old patterns
and don't see an out
once i thought i was moving
but it was only air
passing through me
breaking me apart
like these estranged
vapor clots
lost to heaven's
lonely cognitive activity
down the hill
there's a lo-fi sound system
blasting sentimental bachata
about the interminable
fantasy of modern love

tonight these songs
emancipate the tireless
generator of my debilitating thoughts
it's a sensation i didn't plan for
this useless certitude dissolving
from my gut's habituated knots
i always remember
not wanting to be a person
in the crowd
participating reluctantly
under infinite spasms
of tiny flashing lights
cotton candy boys soliciting
my emotional involvement
amidst an electric throng
of passing people animals and moths
mariana you are only a symbol
but still i did a double take
when i thought i saw you there at dusk
it's just i can never shake you
from my intrapersonal involvements
and this music is so loud so copacetic
it pins my head
in a terminally romantic lock
although it embarrasses me
to say so
the hot pink sunset you missed
was more spectacular

than any hallucination
our love has wrought
now in the aftermath
the clouds are fading
against the atmosphere
in a color
i can only describe

confirmation bias

at least in our waking life
most commemoration
doubles as force

since even
the most benign
zodiacal conceptions
are tinged eurocentric

when brown women die
who specifically is responsible
for the eroticization
of our deaths?

this is not a walking
meditation

not an endorsement
of escape
survivalism
or even
getting to the source

with eyes closed
involve yourself
with the idea

of becoming thematized
                    in dreams
            that feel multiplayer

wearing cling wrap for clothing
            seldom (never) passing
            white

learn to chase dopamine
in the absence of halos

notice what you feel
when your phone
reaches out
for you

notice this as
paradise

notice paradise
as antithetical
to force

notice force
as the catalyst
            for everyone
            you've ever
            loved
            leaving

remember
that you once watched
     someone you love
try to light their cigarette
with a usb stick
          and did nothing
          to intervene

following this memory
you've learned to triple check
fire sources and their
adjacent damage

          if you set an object on fire in the poem
          the poem rewards you by becoming deep

          if you set yourself on fire in the poem
          the poem rewards you for becoming the light

          when you become the light
          the poem says

          ok
          good job

          you've become
          the light

i promise to love
you

notes

milk borrows lines from Science Fiction by Ariana Reines

fire season is lifted from a drunk, post-Trader Joe's conversation with Morgan Blauth

electric hand is imagined through CAConrad's Somatic Rituals from *While Standing in Line for Death*

azul is for my mom, my angel, Elsa

halfway is for Lauren Roth

powerade is dedicated to the Multidisciplinary Association for Psychedelic Studies (MAPS), especially Charlotte Jackson and Hayden Rubensohn

lucifer bitch is for Frodo Baggins

"i promise to love you" was illustrated by Max Babiuk

thanks

thanks to Ashley Obscura and the Metatron family

thanks to Domenica Martinello, my incredible editor

thanks to Marcela Huerta for the beautiful design

thanks to Serisa Fitz-James for the author photo

thanks to my sister, Ludi Leiva—goon, we're doing it

thanks to my dad, my favorite Gemini, Peter Besenovsky, for continual encouragement and laughter

thanks to my mom, Elsa Besenovsky, for unconventional lessons in metaphysics and resiliency—mucho y el corazón

thanks to Aja Moore for catalyzing a transformative love of poetics in me

thanks to Amna Elnour for opulent realness

thanks to Ash Baccus-Clark for unconditional support and bodega snacks thanks to Callie Hitchcock for endless belief and heart advice

thanks to Catie Payne for Piscean wisdom and unparalleled loyalty

thanks to Emily O'Brien for celestial radiance and honesty

thanks to Ernesto Breittmayer for pisco sours and soul lessons

thanks to Evan Jones for midnight cigarettes and listening

thanks to Jon Tastad for being a faithful pen pal and a star beyond all measure

thanks to Jonathan Mak for the gorgeous years we do and don't remember

thanks to Kaitlyn Purcell for smuggling cheesecake and caring

thanks to Lauren Ray for etherealizing my life with creative visions and compassion

thanks to Majestic Ross for being a warm light in all climates thanks to the Mirepoix boys——i love y'all forever

thanks to Molly Short and Tessa Bryant for elevating my faith in friendship

thanks to the Prince Ed duplex angels for being home to me

thanks to Ruffles for gallons of seltzer and shopping cart cries

thanks to Sara Azarshahi for being a second sister and my truest confidante

thanks to Trader Joe's 547 for memes and solidarity

thanks to Xavier Très-Chanceux for beautiful and strange inspiration

thanks to Charlotte Shane, Daniel Borzutzky, Elaine Kahn, and Marwa Helal for your wildly generous words about this book

thanks to Hoa Nguyen, Karen Solie, LA Warman, Tony Tulathimutte, Sheryda Warrener, David O'Meara, Robert Lashley, Ben Fama, Jackie Clark, Adèle Barclay, Fred Moten, Ariana Reines, Dawn Lundy Martin, Jackie Wang, and Anne Boyer for your mentorship thanks to Dr. Tuesday, Tracy, Malikah, Jeannine, and Nancy

thanks to Ludmila and Ludovit Besenovsky who survived and transcended political exile as Slavic refugees— we never met, but i carry with you with me and hope to one day learn to read and translate your poems

thanks to Seattle, Vancouver, Montréal, Guatemala City, Santiago, Bellingham, and Brooklyn for raising me

thanks to the editors at Bedfellows Magazine, Blue Mesa Review, Blush Lit, Columbia Journal, Discorder Magazine, From Bellingham with Love, Girls Club Zine, glitterMOB, Hobart, Metatron Press, Pacific Dissent, Peach Mag, Poetry Is Dead Magazine, Prism International, The Puritan, and Theta Wave, for publishing many of these poems

thanks to my family—the Besenovsky, Fichtner, Leiva, Horáček, Saad, Santamaria, Azarshahi, Ray, Riel, Roth, and Valadez families—los quiero mucho

and all my friends, i love you incredibly, we're so lucky to have found each other in this life

Ivanna Baranova

is a Guatemalan-Slovak writer, editor, and photographer
from the Pacific Northwest. She is a graduate of the
University of British Columbia, with a Bachelor's in
Philosophy, Social Theory, and Creative Writing. She
is a Pisces and currently resides in Brooklyn. Find her
at www.ivannabaranova.com.